American G
SUPREME COURT

John Perritano

M000105536

SADDLEBACK
EDUCATIONAL PUBLISHING

SADDLEBACK HANDBOOK SERIES

AMERICAN GOVERNMENT

Foundations

Office of the President

Congress

Supreme Court

Political Parties

Photo credits: Page 21: Alamy.com; page 26: Alamy.com; page: 38; page 40/41: Alamy.com; page 44: Neftali / Shutterstock.com; page 45: Joseph Sohm / Shutterstock.com; page 46: Atomazul / Shutterstock.com; page 50: Everett Historical / Shutterstock.com; page 51: Joseph Sohm / Shutterstock.com; page 55: Alamy.com; page 55: Rob Crandall / Shutterstock.com; page 59: Everett Historical / Shutterstock.com; page 61: Alamy.com; page 71: Boris Stroujko / Shutterstock.com; page 74/75: Rena Schild / Shutterstock.com; page 77: eugenio Marongiu / Shutterstock.com; page 80: Alamy.com; page 81: John Kropewnicki / Shutterstock.com; all other images from Shutterstock.com

SADDLEBACK
EDUCATIONAL PUBLISHING
www.sdlback.com

ISBN-13: 978-1-68021-119-1
ISBN-10: 1-68021-119-6
eBook: 978-1-63078-434-8

Printed in Guangzhou, China
NOR/0216/CA21600190

20 19 18 17 16 1 2 3 4 5

TABLE OF CONTENTS

EQUAL·JUSTICE

Introduction

"Equal justice under law." What does it mean? The words are written on a building. The building is in Washington, D.C. It's the Supreme Court. Judges work there. They make decisions about the law. The court says if a law is legal. It looks at the Constitution. The court's **rulings** have changed history. Decisions can last a lifetime.

The court has nine **justices**. The most senior is the chief justice. Four women and 108 men have been justices. This includes 17 chief justices. The president gives them their jobs. Justices have their jobs for life. Some retire. Most don't. William O. Douglas worked for 36 years. He retired in 1975.

Some justices stood out. Others didn't have much to say. Can you name a Supreme Court justice? Most Americans can't.

John Marshall

How about past justices? Like John Marshall. He was the fourth chief justice. Marshall worked for 34 years. (*1801–1835*) He served the longest as chief justice. Marshall started an idea. It's called **judicial review**. The court can say laws are not legal. Unconstitutional. It is a way to balance power.

Roger B. Taney

Roger B. Taney was a chief justice too. It was in 1857. Not everyone was treated fairly. The court made a bad ruling. It said slaves were not citizens. Nor could they ever be citizens. But the laws changed. How? There was the Civil War. And later two amendments were passed.

Earl Warren was the 14th chief justice. (*1953–1969*) Warren said, "Separate educational facilities are **inherently** unequal." All people had to be treated the same. **Racism** was not legal.

Today three women are justices. There are six men. Five of the current justices went to Harvard Law School. Three went to Yale Law School. And one went to Columbia Law School. There are few skills needed for the job. But everyone who has served has been a lawyer.

Presidents come and go, but the Supreme Court goes on forever.
—William Howard Taft

Chapter 1
THE SUPREMES ROCK

William Howard Taft knew about service. Taft was a U.S. president. He was also a Supreme Court justice. Taft was the only president to serve on the court. He liked being a judge. "I love judges, and I love courts. They are my ideals, that typify on earth what we shall meet hereafter in heaven under a just God," he said.

It was 1921. Warren G. Harding was president. He made Taft chief justice of the United States. Taft improved the court. He organized it. Taft worked to pass a law. It was the Judiciary Act of

William Howard Taft

1925. The court could now decide which cases to hear. Taft wrote over 200 opinions. He also swore in two presidents. Taft gave the oath of office. First was Calvin Coolidge. Next was Herbert Hoover.

Becoming chief justice was Taft's dream. He loved the Supreme Court. It is the highest court in the land. The court is part of the third branch of government. It is called the judiciary.

LEGISLATIVE
Makes Laws

EXECUTIVE
Carries Out Laws

JUDICIAL
Interprets Laws

The judiciary shares power with Congress. It also

shares power with the president. The framers wrote the rules. They wrote the Constitution. It's a great document. It spells out how the government should work. But not much is written about the courts. There are less than 400 words. The courts were the weakest part of government.

The courts needed to run themselves. Judges should not be controlled. Not by the public. And not by lawmakers. Their job is to decide cases. It's not about making people happy or being popular. That's why all federal judges have their jobs for life.

Think About It: *Should federal judges have their jobs for life?*

[FINAL SAY]

The Supreme Court has the final say on the law. The judges don't all have to agree. The majority decides the law. Everyone must follow it. Congress. And the president too.

MAJOR CIVIL RIGHTS CASES

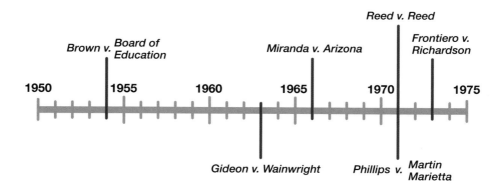

The court has changed millions of lives with its rulings.

- Separate but equal schools was not legal. (*Brown v. Board of Education*)
- States must provide a lawyer to anyone facing trial. (*Gideon v. Wainwright*)
- If arrested, people must be told their rights. This happens before police can question them. (*Miranda v. Arizona*)

There have been changes in women's rights too.

- Laws that treat women unfairly are not legal. (*Reed v. Reed*)

- Employers cannot refuse to hire mothers with young children. (*Phillips v. Martin Marietta*)
- The military gives out benefits to families of its members. Those benefits cannot be awarded differently because of sex. (*Frontiero v. Richardson*)

[STATE COURTS]

The U.S. government is a federal system. Power is divided. It is shared. The national government has power. But it shares power with the states. The same is true for the courts. Power is shared. There are federal courts and state courts. They hear different kinds of cases. State courts hear cases about everyday laws. They can be about crimes. Broken traffic laws. Family law.

CASES FOR STATE COURTS

STATE COURTS

- Family law issues
- Criminal matters
- Wills and trusts
- Property disputes

Each state court is an expert. It knows its own laws and rules. It also looks for meaning in the U.S. Constitution. Those rulings may be **appealed**. That's where the U.S. Supreme Court comes in.

[U.S. COURTS]

Article III of the Constitution. "The judicial Power of the United States shall be vested in one Supreme Court," it says. And "Congress may from time to time ordain and establish" lower courts.

Federal courts have three levels. Congress made these courts. It sets the number of judges in each court. And Congress says what kinds of cases the courts will hear. It also sets the budget. The president picks judges. Congress okays them.

[DISTRICT COURTS]

District courts are trial courts. A judge tries cases. Juries decide cases. There are other judges.

Called magistrates. They help get the cases ready for trial.

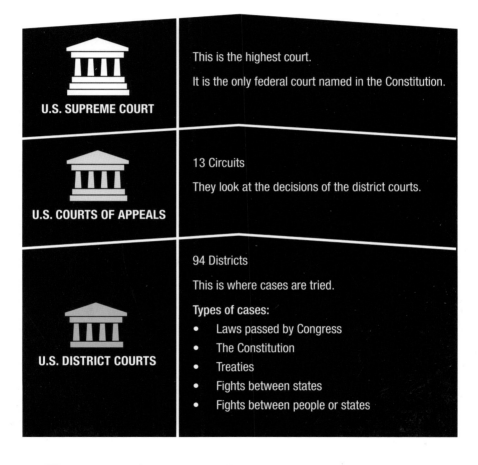

U.S. SUPREME COURT

This is the highest court.

It is the only federal court named in the Constitution.

U.S. COURTS OF APPEALS

13 Circuits

They look at the decisions of the district courts.

U.S. DISTRICT COURTS

94 Districts

This is where cases are tried.

Types of cases:
- Laws passed by Congress
- The Constitution
- Treaties
- Fights between states
- Fights between people or states

There is at least one district court in each state. There is also one in the District of Columbia. Each U.S. territory has one too. This includes Puerto Rico,

U.S. TERRITORY DISTRICT COURT MAP

the Virgin Islands, Guam, and the Northern Mariana Islands. Each district has a special court. It is a bankruptcy court. It decides if a person has to pay what they owe.

The president picks district court judges. They can be lawyers. Or they can be state or local judges. Congress has to okay them. There are over 670 district court judges.

[COURTS OF APPEALS]

The courts of appeals are circuit courts. There are

13 circuits. Circuit courts can hear any type of case. Each court can have many judges. Some have six. One has 29. There is a senior judge for each circuit. The senior judge usually runs the court.

The president gives the judges their jobs. Congress has to give its okay. Judges have their jobs for life. All current justices have been judges. They worked in the U.S. courts of appeals. Except Elena Kagan. She was **solicitor general**. Kagan was also dean of Harvard Law School.

Each appeals court can change a district court's ruling. That's what happened with Barry Bonds. He was a professional baseball player. Federal police arrested him. They said he lied about using drugs. The drugs helped him play better. They were not legal.

A district court found Bonds guilty. The case went to the Ninth Circuit. It is an appeals court.

A group of three judges ruled against Bonds. His lawyers appealed. They wanted more judges to hear the case.

Ninth Circuit Court of Appeals

This time eleven judges heard it. The court ruled for Barry Bonds. It **overturned** the district court's guilty **verdict**.

Three judges usually hear appeals cases. There are no witnesses. No jury is called. What is the court's job? To see if the district court used the law correctly. The appeals court can overturn a ruling if not. It can send the case back to the district court. There would be a new trial.

What if a person doesn't like a circuit court's ruling? There is only one place to go. The case goes to the Supreme Court.

U.S. COURTS OF APPEALS 13 CIRCUITS		
District of Columbia	John G. Roberts Jr., chief justice	District of Columbia
First Circuit	Stephen Breyer, associate justice	First Circuit: Maine, Massachusetts, New Hampshire, Puerto Rico, Rhode Island
Second Circuit	Ruth Bader Ginsburg, associate justice	Connecticut, New York, Vermont
Third Circuit	Samuel A. Alito Jr., associate justice	Delaware, New Jersey, Pennsylvania, Virgin Islands
Fourth Circuit	John G. Roberts Jr., chief justice	Maryland, North Carolina, South Carolina, Virginia, West Virginia
Fifth Circuit	Antonin Scalia, associate justice	Louisiana, Mississippi, Texas
Sixth Circuit	Elena Kagan, associate justice	Kentucky, Michigan, Ohio, Tennessee
Seventh Circuit	Elena Kagan, associate justice	Illinois, Indiana, Wisconsin
Eighth Circuit	Samuel A. Alito Jr., associate justice	Arkansas, Iowa, Minnesota, Missouri, Nebraska, North Dakota, South Dakota
Ninth Circuit	Anthony M. Kennedy, associate justice	Alaska, Arizona, California, Guam, Hawaii, Idaho, Montana, Nevada, Northern Mariana Islands, Oregon, Washington
Tenth Circuit	Sonia Sotomayor, associate justice	Colorado, Kansas, New Mexico, Oklahoma, Utah, Wyoming
Eleventh Circuit	Clarence Thomas, associate justice	Alabama, Florida, Georgia
Federal Circuit	John G. Roberts Jr., chief justice	All Federal Judicial Districts

[THE HIGHEST COURT]

The Supreme Court is the top federal court. Its decisions are final. The Supreme Court can say which laws are not legal. How does a case get there? It begins with a decision from a lower court. A person is unhappy with it. They decide to appeal. The Supreme Court is asked to hear the case. The court may agree. It orders the lower court to send the files. This is called a **writ of certiorari**. The court will look at the case.

WRIT OF CERTIORARI
Sent for Review and Consideration

U.S. SUPREME COURT
Decides Which Laws Are Illegal

Nine judges sit on the court. They are called justices. One is the chief justice. The others are associate justices. All serve until they die or retire. Or they can be removed from office for a crime.

Congress sets the number of judges. In 1789, there were six. There have been as many as 10. The fewest number was five. The current number was set in 1869.

Justices hear cases. But they also have other jobs. Each justice directs at least one federal circuit. A justice may be asked to stop an execution. Justices have other circuit duties too. Justice Kennedy is in charge of the Ninth Circuit. Chief Justice Roberts heads three circuits. The Federal Circuit. The District of Columbia. And the Fourth Circuit.

Justice Kennedy

The Supreme Court first met in New York City. It was in 1790. Only three justices were there. Not enough for an official meeting. That happened the next day. John Jay was the chief justice. There were five associate justices. James Wilson. William Cushing. John Blair. John Rutledge. James Iredell.

The chief justice is the boss. He is the first to enter the courtroom. The first to vote. But his vote is no greater than the others. The chief justice assigns the **majority opinions**. What if the chief justice is in the minority? The most senior justice in the majority assigns the opinion.

The majority opinion says the court's ruling. It also gives the reasons for it. Reasons are backed up by the rules of law. The justices who agreed with the ruling sign the opinion. Opinions are published. They can be found in the *United States Reports*.

Most Supreme Court decisions are under 5,000 words. A decision gives the facts of the case. Then comes the court's opinion and the action. The Supreme Court can agree with the lower court. It can reverse the lower court's ruling. Or the court can send the case back to the lower court. There will be a new trial.

ACTIONS OF THE SUPREME COURT	
✓	Agree with Lower Court's Ruling
↰	Disagree with Lower Court's Ruling and Reverse It
⧉	Send Back to Lower Court for New Trial

[SHARING POWER]

The Supreme Court shares power with Congress. It also shares power with the president. That is on purpose. No one branch should have too much power. Each branch checks the power of the others. The court checks Congress. It decides if laws are legal. The court checks the executive branch. It decides if its actions are legal.

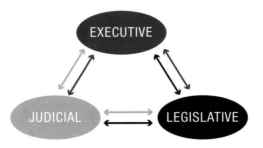

EXECUTIVE

JUDICIAL

LEGISLATIVE

The other branches can check the power of the courts. One way is for the president to pick all federal judges. The president gives judges their jobs. Judges don't have to have a law degree. In the past, some have been congressmen. Others were senators. A few were governors. Some were judges. One was a former president. Congress okays them. It can also reject them.

The House of Representatives can also impeach a federal judge. It is a charge for doing something wrong. It does not mean the judge will be fired. That is up to the Senate. It holds a separate trial to decide guilt.

Only one Supreme Court justice has been impeached. It was Samuel Chase. The House charged Chase with playing favorites. Chase was a Federalist. It was a political party. The justice had a big personality. He often spoke about his political views. Chase said he was being charged for his views. There was no real crime. The Senate agreed. It found Chase not guilty. The decision helped protect judges from lawmakers.

Congress can undo a Supreme Court ruling. How? It can rewrite the law. Or it can pass a new one. Congress did that in 1991. It passed a new **civil rights** law. The law **overrode** five Supreme Court decisions. Those opinions limited the rights of workers. Congress passed the new law to protect workers.

HOW CONGRESS OVERRIDES THE SUPREME COURT

U.S. Supreme Court Overrules Law → **Congress Rewrites/ Creates New Law** → **Law Is Revised**

One case was in 1989. (*Wards Cove Packing Co. v. Atonio*) White workers had skilled jobs. Nonwhite workers had unskilled jobs. The minority workers said it was because of race. The Supreme Court said workers had to prove it. Were they being treated unfairly on purpose? Congress said no. The burden of proof should not be on the workers. Congress changed the law.

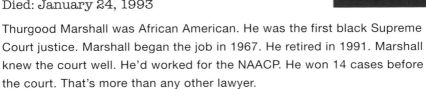

FACES IN THE CROWD

Thurgood Marshall
Born: July 2, 1908
Died: January 24, 1993

Thurgood Marshall was African American. He was the first black Supreme Court justice. Marshall began the job in 1967. He retired in 1991. Marshall knew the court well. He'd worked for the NAACP. He won 14 cases before the court. That's more than any other lawyer.

Brown v. Board of Education was one case. It helped end separate but equal in public schools. The justice believed in civil rights. He voted to limit police searches. Marshall thought the death penalty was wrong. He also supported free speech.

→ HISTORY HAPPENED HERE

Event: *Tinker v. Des Moines*

Who: John and Mary Beth Tinker

When: February 24, 1969

There was a war. It was in Vietnam. Students were against it. They planned a protest. It would be silent. The students would wear black armbands to school. The principal found out. He said no armbands. The students would be in trouble. Get suspended. But the kids did it. And they got in trouble.

Their parents sued. Kids had a right to free speech, they said. That right was violated. A district court agreed with the school. They said the protest could disturb learning. The appeals court agreed. The case then went to the Supreme Court.

It was 1969. The Supreme Court agreed with the students. The decision was 7–2. The court said the students had rights. This included the right to free speech. Rights should be protected. Even when the students were in school.

Chapter 2
JUDICIAL REVIEW

Think of a basketball game. The Supreme Court is the referee. Other parts of government are the players. Some of the players can pass laws. Congress can pass laws. State legislatures can too. Other players enforce laws. The president, governors, and mayors can do this. Everyone has to play by the same set of rules. Rules are in the Constitution.

The Supreme Court can say when any of these players makes a mistake. It decides what actions are against the rules.

It's a process called judicial review. And it was never part of the Constitution. No laws can go against the document. But there's a catch. The Supreme Court can only review laws in cases that are brought to them.

[THIRD WHEEL]

The Supreme Court didn't have much power. It couldn't decide if a law was legal. It first met in 1790. The justices didn't have much to do. They were not asked to rule on any cases. No important decisions were made. It all changed in 1803. That's when the court gave itself its power. It is the most important court case in U.S. history.

John Adams was president. His term was ending. He did not win a second term. But there was still much to do. Adams wanted to pick judges he liked. He wanted to fill the courts with men from his party. Adams was a Federalist. It was a political party.

One of his supporters was William Marbury. Adams made Marbury a justice of the peace. Justices of the peace oversaw small court cases. Adams gave Marbury the job. But the official letter was never sent.

John Adams

The secretary of state was supposed to give Marbury the letter. But he left that job to the new secretary. That was James Madison. President Adams's secretary of state was John Marshall. The future chief justice.

Enter Thomas Jefferson. He was the new president. Adams and Jefferson did not like each other. One day Jefferson visited the State Department. He saw some letters on a table. He knew what they were. They were the official letters signed by Adams. One was for Marbury.

Thomas Jefferson   James Madison

[A MAJOR CASE]

Jefferson ordered James Madison not to send any letters. Nobody would get their job. Marbury was mad. He said he had a right to his new job. The job was his even without the letter. He asked the Supreme Court for help. Force Madison to send him the letter, he said.

The court took the case. It was called *Marbury v. Madison*. John Marshall was the chief justice. He was also Jefferson's distant cousin. A cousin Jefferson did not like. Jefferson's allies were upset that the court took the case. The executive branch

The Supreme Court's first session was in 1790. Justice William Cushing arrived. He came into the courtroom. He wore a white wig. Judges in England wore them. So did judges in the American colonies. But the U.S. was a new country. It wasn't under English rule any longer. Judges in the U.S. left their wigs at home. Except Cushing. He wanted to keep the tradition alive. People made fun of him. Thomas Jefferson even said the wig made judges look like rats.

refused to help the court. It slowed down the work.

The court gave a ruling. It blamed Jefferson and Madison. It said they did not follow the law. The men had no right to not send the letters. The court said that Marbury was hired. He had a legal right to his job.

Then the court said something else. It talked about a law Congress passed. It was the Judiciary Act of 1789. The law was against the Constitution. Marbury used that law. He filed his lawsuit with the Supreme Court. He skipped over other courts. The court said no. Marbury could not file his lawsuit. At least not with the Supreme Court. The court said it couldn't hear the case. The Constitution did give it the power to hear cases. But *only* on appeal from other courts.

So Marshall said Marbury deserved his job. But he also said the court could do nothing about it. Congress had passed the law. But it went against the Constitution. Marbury made a mistake. He'd asked the court to look at his case. He never asked lower courts. And that was wrong.

It was historic. The first time a law was called not legal. Unconstitutional. An idea was born. It is called judicial review.

[EQUAL IN POWER]

The court also said something else. It could look at the actions of the federal government. It could even look at the actions of state governments. Marshall said it was the job of the courts "to say what the law is."

The court gave itself the power to reject laws. It made the court powerful. The court was equal to the other branches.

Marbury v. Madison, *judicial review was born*

Marbury never got his job. He was owed it. Adams had given it to him. The court agreed. However, it said the final decision was Jefferson's.

The court's independence was set. Marshall ignored political pressure. The Federalists wanted Jefferson to hand over the letters. They wanted the court to make him do it. This would embarrass the president. Jefferson's party was firm. They would not follow the court's rule. The party liked state courts.

Marshall said both sides were right. He said Jefferson owed Marbury the job. But he also said the court could do nothing. It could not legally make the president do anything.

Marshall believed the courts should be independent. It was important for the growing country. He made the three branches of government equal in power.

It was 54 years before another law was called illegal.

[IN ACTION]

Alexander Hamilton didn't think much of the court. He said it was "next to nothing."

John Marshall proved Hamilton wrong. By establishing judicial review, Marshall changed the court. Here are some examples.

It was 1989. Congress passed a law. It said citizens could not burn the American flag. The Supreme Court said the law was wrong. The law went against the right to free speech. (*United States v. Eichman*)

Alexander Hamilton

The city of Ladue, Missouri, had a law against yard signs. Margaret Gilleo placed a sign in her front yard. The sign was a protest. Gilleo was against the first Gulf War. The city asked her to remove it. Gilleo sued. She said the city violated her right to free speech. The Supreme Court agreed. (*Ladue v. Gilleo*)

Pole taxes were against the law. They were not legal in national elections. But Virginia still had the tax. It was for local elections. How was the tax collected? People had to pay money to register to vote. Annie Harper could not afford it. She sued.

The case went to the Supreme Court. The court said Virginia broke the law. The state violated the 14th Amendment. It did not give Harper equal protection. All people should be able to vote. Income should not matter. (*Harper v. Virginia Board of Elections*)

Judicial review even upset a president. President Richard M. Nixon refused to hand over tape recordings. It was for an investigation. Nixon stated "absolute executive privilege." The Supreme Court said no.

Richard M. Nixon

Nixon's words were rejected. The president quit weeks after the decision. (*United States v. Nixon*)

FACES IN THE CROWD

John Marshall
Born: September 24, 1755
Died: July 6, 1835

John Marshall was the most important chief justice. The Marbury case was key. Marshall helped decide more than 1,000 court cases. He wrote more than 500 opinions. Marshall's image even appeared on the $500 bill in 1918.

Marshall was born in Virginia. He was the first of 15 children. One of his classmates was James Monroe. Monroe would become the fifth president. Marshall fought in the Revolutionary War.

Marshall studied law at the College of William and Mary. The college is in Williamsburg, Virginia. He began his own practice. Marshall even helped with the U.S. Constitution.

Marshall died at age 79 in Philadelphia, Pennsylvania.

Chapter 3
CASELOAD

Some 10,000 cases reach the court each year. Most are appeals from lower courts. Lawyers for those cases file a request. It's the writ of certiorari. The Supreme Court cannot hear every case. They have to choose a few. The justices meet in secret. They decide which cases to hear. There is a "rule of four." Four justices agree. Then a case can come before the court. The justices grant the writ. They never explain why they take cases. No one except the justices ever knows the reasons.

A justice may disagree with a decision to reject a case. They can issue a statement. It says why the case should be heard. It's called a "Term Opinion Relating to Orders."

The court can only hear cases involving federal law. It can also decide to look at other cases. But only those that fall within the control of federal courts. Those cases can include crimes on federal land. Cases can also involve fights between states.

The court cannot hear any issue about state law. That is the job of state courts. The court also hears cases when lower courts ignore its rulings. A lower court may decide a ruling does not apply. Or a lower court may think a ruling is not clear.

What if federal courts have different rulings on the same issue? The court will also hear those cases. Same-sex marriage was one of those cases. The court will also hear cases a justice might like.

But a justice has to convince three others to hear the case.

Which cases to take? Those decisions can send shockwaves across the country. Such was a 1956 case from Alabama. A tired woman took a bus ride that changed history.

Think About It: *Thurgood Marshall called the Constitution "a realistic document of freedom." But only after "corrective amendments" were added. Did the original Constitution discriminate against groups of people?*

[TIRED OF GIVING IN]

It was December 1, 1955. Rosa Parks had just left work. She was a seamstress in Montgomery, Alabama. Parks got on a city bus. She headed home.

African Americans could not sit just anywhere. They were not allowed to sit in seats marked "Whites Only." It was against the law.

Other seats could fill up. Then drivers ordered black riders to stand.

More white passengers got on that night. African Americans had to give up their seats. Parks said no. She would not stand. Rosa Parks was "tired of giving in."

[BOYCOTT]

The bus driver called the police. The police came. They arrested her. Parks was taken to city hall. She was charged. Parks had broken the city's segregation laws.

The bus Rosa Parks sat in

The arrest made African Americans angry. Mrs. Parks stood before a judge four days later. He found her guilty of breaking a city law. He fined her $10. There was also a $4 charge for court costs.

African Americans quickly organized. There was a **boycott** of the city's buses. They refused to ride the buses any longer. A young Baptist minister led them. His name was Martin Luther King Jr.

Martin Luther King Jr. National Memorial in Washington, D.C.

The boycott went on. It lasted for more than a year. Montgomery's black residents walked. They carpooled. But they didn't take the bus.

[THE COURT ACTS]

Parks's case made its way through the courts. She appealed her conviction. Finally the Supreme Court agreed to hear the case.

It was November 1956. The justices made a decision. Racial segregation on buses in Montgomery was illegal. Many laws throughout the South were now illegal. All the justices agreed. It was unanimous. The next day Parks boarded a city bus. She sat at the front.

Parks's brave action helped the civil rights movement. But there was a **backlash**. Mr. and Mrs. Parks got death threats. They were fired from their jobs. There were hate calls. It was 1957. They left the South for good. It took almost a decade for Rosa Parks to find steady work. She worked for a congressman from 1965–1988. Rosa Parks died in 2005.

[CORRECTING MISTAKES]

Stare decisis. It means "let the decision stand."
Lower courts must accept higher court decisions.
Changing a past Supreme Court decision is hard.
But it can be done. One way is to amend the
Constitution. Another way is for the Supreme Court
to overrule itself. This has happened. How? Other
cases have been brought before the court. Those
cases have the same questions. But many years
have passed. Times have changed. The court
changes its mind.

Dred Scott v. Sandford is a famous case in U.S.
history. In a 6–3 decision, the court said that slaves
could not be U.S. citizens. Their children could not
be citizens either. It said something else. People
with African blood could not sue in federal court.
The Fifth Amendment protected slave owners, it
said. This was because slaves were "property."
Two constitutional amendments fixed this ruling.
The 13th Amendment ended slavery. The 14th

Amendment gave citizenship to all former slaves.

Dred Scott

Courts said no to interracial marriage. (*Pace v. Alabama*) Blacks could not marry whites. Whites could not marry blacks. The Supreme Court agreed. It said the law was not unfair. The punishment was the same for whites and blacks. It was 1967. The law was finally overturned. (*Loving v. Virginia*) The court said those laws were illegal. It said the laws were racist. People of any race were free to marry.

The South passed laws. Called Jim Crow laws. (*Plessy v. Ferguson*) The laws limited the rights of African Americans. Homer Plessy was one-eighth

African. He rode in the white section of a train. Then he stated his ancestry. He was asked to move. Plessy refused. He was arrested. The case went to the Supreme Court. It didn't believe having separate sections for blacks and whites was illegal. It ruled against Plessy. Separate but equal became the rule. The case was finally overturned. (*Brown v. Board of Education*) Separate was not equal.

HISTORY HAPPENED HERE

Event: *Bush v. Gore*

Where: The Supreme Court

When: 2000

It was 2000. There was a presidential election. But it was not over on Election Day. No one knew who won. Was it Al Gore? Was it George Bush? Voting ended on November 7. The results were in from every state except Florida. Whoever won Florida would win the election. Florida's Supreme Court ordered officials to count the ballots again. Bush did not want that to happen. Gore might win the state. If that happened, Gore would become president.

Bush asked the Supreme Court to stop the recount. Some justices did not want to hear the case. They said it wasn't the court's job. Courts should not interfere in elections. But four justices wanted to hear the case.

It was December 1. Bush's lawyers spoke. Gore's lawyers spoke. The court voted. It was December 12. It sided with Bush. It was a 5–4 vote. There would be no recount. Bush won Florida's electors. He won the presidency too.

SUPREME COURT | 51

Chapter 4
FIRST MONDAY IN OCTOBER

It's the first Monday in October. A term of the Supreme Court begins. It continues until late June. Justices hear cases. They give opinions.

It's 10:00 a.m. The marshal of the Supreme Court bangs a gavel. "Oyez! Oyez! Oyez!" the marshal shouts. "All persons having business before the Honorable, the Supreme Court of the United States, are **admonished** to draw near and give their attention, for the Court is now sitting. God save the United States and this Honorable Court."

The justices enter the courtroom. The chief justice is first. He moves to the center of a big desk. It's called the bench. The other justices follow. Some stand close to the chief justice. They have been on the court the longest. Others stand at the ends. They have been there the least amount of time.

The justices sit. Then everyone else sits too.

Think About It: *Ruth Bader Ginsburg is a Supreme Court justice. Ginsburg hopes that dissents can change people's minds. Do dissenting opinions become majority opinions over time?*

[OFF TO WORK]

The court gets to work. But it is not like other courts. There are no witnesses. No juries. It's just the justices and lawyers. Each lawyer represents one side of a case. Each side has about 30 minutes to talk. They say why their view is right. These are called oral arguments.

Justice Thomas

The justices ask questions. Some justices may not ask any. Clarence Thomas is a Supreme Court justice. He became one in 1991. He is known for rarely asking a question.

Often you can tell what a justice is thinking. How? By the questions they ask. Sometimes you can't tell. But lawyers have to be quick on their feet. They have to be ready to answer. Their case depends on it.

Lawyers don't want the justices to ask too many questions. That's what one reporter said. The case will be lost. This is because a justice has doubts. They ask many questions.

[TAKING A SEAT]

The public can watch what goes on in the courtroom. It's first come, first seated. Some are special guests of the justices. They sit on benches to the right of the justices. There is also a row of black chairs. They are saved for retired justices. Officers of the court also sit there.

THE SUPREME COURT SEATING CHART

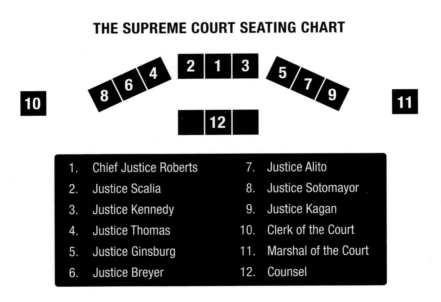

1.	Chief Justice Roberts	7.	Justice Alito
2.	Justice Scalia	8.	Justice Sotomayor
3.	Justice Kennedy	9.	Justice Kagan
4.	Justice Thomas	10.	Clerk of the Court
5.	Justice Ginsburg	11.	Marshal of the Court
6.	Justice Breyer	12.	Counsel

There is a clerk of the Supreme Court. The clerk sits to the left of the justices. Their job is to give the justices any papers they might need. The marshal sits on the right of the courtroom. The marshal records what is said. The marshal also keeps time. Lawyers cannot go over the limit. The marshal handles court security too. The current marshal of the Supreme Court is Pamela Talkin. She is the first woman to hold the job. Ms. Talkin used to be a high school teacher.

[LEGAL BRIEFS]

A case is accepted. It is scheduled. The justices don't rely just on what the lawyers say. Both sides give briefs. Briefs are legal papers. Papers have to be written in a certain way. They state the facts of the case. Why is the case before the court? A brief supports a legal position. It tells the judges what the case is about. It also gives reasons to rule one way or another.

Briefs can't be longer than 50 pages. The side asking for the hearing sends a brief. That side is called the petitioner. The other side can reply in a brief. That side is called the respondent. Shorter briefs can be filed too. Those briefs respond to each side's position. The government also can file a brief. But only if it is not part of the case.

Some people send a friend-of-the-court brief. All want the justices to think about the case. Friends of the court are not part of the case either.

[SIMILAR CASES]

The lawyers talk about similar cases in their briefs. These are called **precedents**. The Supreme Court's decisions set precedents. All other courts must follow them. No lower court can give a different ruling. Lower courts cannot go against a Supreme Court decision. The court relies on past rulings in deciding cases.

The court can overturn its own decision. It happened in *Brown v. Board of Education.* It allowed African American children and white children to go to the same school. The ruling overturned *Plessy v. Ferguson*.

States can overturn a decision. They do it by adding to the Constitution. It's called amending. Two-thirds of states must agree. It's not easy. But it has happened several times. The Dred Scott ruling was overturned. But it took two amendments. Those passed after the Civil War. The 13th Amendment ended slavery. The 14th Amendment made all former slaves U.S. citizens.

[CHANGING THE LAW]

Adding to the Constitution is hard. Drafting new laws may be easier. That is what Congress did in 1986. The Supreme Court struck down a law. The law helped disabled people. It protected them from being treated unfairly. The court said the law did not apply to airlines. Congress passed a new law. It didn't overturn the court's decision. But it did protect the rights of disabled people.

Lilly Ledbetter was the only woman employee in her group. She was given low raises. Male workers earned more money. Ledbetter sued. (*Ledbetter v. Goodyear Tire and Rubber Co.*) She said Goodyear violated Title VII. It was part of a civil rights law.

A jury awarded her over $3.5 million. Goodyear appealed. It said the suit had to be filed earlier. There was a time limit. It was 180 days.

The appeals court agreed. It sided with the company. Goodyear did not treat Ledbetter unfairly. In the 180 days after her last review, the company was fair. The court dropped the case. Ledbetter asked the Supreme Court for help. It ruled against her too. The words of Title VII set a time limit.

ON THE JOB

It was the 1970s. Ruth Bader Ginsburg was a lawyer. She worked for the ACLU. Ginsburg set up the Women's Rights Project. She wanted more opportunities for women. Six of her cases went before the Supreme Court. She won five of them.

It was 2009. A bill was signed. Called the Lilly Ledbetter Fair Pay Act. The new law made one thing clear. Each paycheck could be an act of unfair treatment. Each act could be tested in court. President Obama signed the bill. "We are all created equal," he said. He also said everyone deserves a chance at happiness.

Event: Editing a High School
Newspaper

Who: Catherine Kuhlmeier,
High School Student

When: 1983

Catherine Kuhlmeier was a high school student. She was also a reporter. Catherine wrote for the school paper. There was a deadline. Students were about to publish two articles. One about teen pregnancy. The other about divorce. In the divorce article, one girl blamed her father for her parents' breakup.

The writers protected everyone's privacy. They used fake names. The principal wanted changes made. Parents had not been given a chance to respond. But there was no time. It was the last edition of the paper. School would be over for the year. So the principal killed the stories. The students took the school to court. Was their right to free speech violated?

It was 1988. The Supreme Court said no. It said the school sponsored the paper. Stories had to be appropriate. The school had the right to decide what was printed.

Chapter 5
DECISION TIME

The oral arguments are over. All the legal briefs are in. What happens next? The justices return to their offices. These are their chambers. They prepare to decide the case. The justices think about what they've heard. They read the briefs from each side. The justices also review law books. Now they are ready to make an informed decision.

Supreme Court cases are decided in private. No one knows what goes on when the justices meet. But Justice Alito gave an interview once. He spoke of what happens.

The justices meet on the Friday after they hear the cases. They sit around a table. The justices discuss what happened. The chief justice speaks first. He tells the others what he believes should happen.

Each of the others then speak. They go in order. From the first to join the court to the last. The justices each tell how they will vote.

The Supreme Court can agree with a lower court's ruling. The ruling stands. Or the court can disagree with the lower court. It can reverse the ruling. The case may go back to the lower court. There will be a new trial or hearing.

Think About It: *President Ulysses S. Grant had a thought. Nobody can say what the future holds. Some things can't be predicted. Different times need different rules. Do the laws from 100 years ago work today?*

[EVERYONE'S OPINION]

The court explains its decisions. It writes an opinion. There are several kinds.

MAJORITY More justices agree than disagree. Tells why the ruling was made.

CONCURRING Justices agree with the majority. But they have different reasons. The opinion says why.

DISSENTING Written by justices in the minority. Says why they disagree with the majority.

PLURALITY The majority of justices agree. But they have different reasons. No opinion has full support. But one gets more support than any other.

MEMORANDUM The justices all agree. The opinion gives only the decision. No reasons are given.

Not all justices have the same views. They don't see the Constitution the same way. Some say it should be followed word for word. It has a strict meaning. Justice Scalia once said that the Constitution is not a living thing. "It's a legal document," he said. "It says what it says and doesn't say what it doesn't say."

Other justices have a different view. They say the document is living. It should change with the times. No one could know what the modern world would be like. The words should work for today. These justices think about each case. There is more to it than the words in the law. They decide what is best for the people.

[STRICT]

Justice Scalia joined the court in 1986. He believes the Constitution has a set meaning. Look at the original words. They help judges as they rule. Scalia is uneasy. Justices may ignore the document. They will switch the words with what they think is right. Scalia believes "Words have meaning. And their meaning doesn't change."

[EVERYDAY]

Justice Breyer joined the court in 1994. He believes in a living Constitution. Breyer's worry is that the values are old. They may no longer work for today. The values must be shaped to make sense. Breyer talks about communication. The way we speak is always changing. Ideas like freedom

ON THE JOB

Cases are heard from October to April. They are open to the public. Each case is given one hour. Each side has only 30 minutes to present its case. The justices spend most of that time asking questions.

of speech and right to privacy have new meaning.

[MIDDLE GROUND]

Justices agree on one thing. They think about their words. All judges have that job.

[CHANGING MINDS]

The justices write their opinions. But they can change their minds. That's what happened in 1992. There was one case. It was about praying in school. A rabbi was asked to speak at a middle school graduation.

A parent did not want the rabbi to speak. He believed it was not right. It was against freedom of religion. Public schools cannot favor one religion over another.

The graduation went on. The rabbi prayed. Then everyone left. But the case didn't go away. It went to the Supreme Court.

Was it okay for the rabbi to pray? The court said yes. Justice Kennedy voted with the majority. He was asked to write the opinion. But then he changed his mind. Kennedy still wrote the majority opinion. Praying at the school was not right. It went against the First Amendment.

[LANDMARK DECISIONS]

Not every Supreme Court ruling is historic. But there are **landmark** cases. They have changed how people think and act. Government works differently because of them. New laws are created.

The court usually decides similar cases the same way. That's why landmark cases are rare. You have already read about some of them. *Marbury v. Madison*. *Dred Scott v. Sandford*. *Plessy v. Ferguson*. *Brown v. Board of Education*.

One big decision was given in 2015. Maybe you have heard about it.

HISTORY HAPPENED HERE

Event: The Swearing-In of Two Justices

Who: Lewis F. Powell Jr. and William H. Rehnquist

When: January 7, 1972

Each justice has a place to sit. Where is based on how long they've served. This is called seniority. But something rare happened. It was on January 7, 1972. Two justices joined the court on that day. Lewis F. Powell Jr. was sworn in. So was William H. Rehnquist. Who was the senior judge? It was Powell. Why? Age was a factor. Powell was 64. Rehnquist was 47.

Powell was from Virginia. Rehnquist was from Wisconsin. Both men were asked to serve by President Nixon.

Chapter 6
DUE PROCESS

The justices of the Supreme Court sat. They listened. It was for over two hours. Some asked questions. Others did not.

The nine justices had a choice to make. It was a matter of changing the law. Should same-sex couples be able to marry? It was April 28, 2015. The court would decide two months later. The matter would be settled. Years of court fights would come to an end.

Several states did not allow the couples to marry. A few couples took those states to court. They said the states were breaking the law. The states were denying them their civil rights. Civil rights are basic. They include the right to vote. To be treated fairly by the law is another right. The cases started in federal district courts. Some judges ruled for the couples. Others ruled for the states.

The Supreme Court stepped in to stop the fight. It would decide if same-sex marriage was legal.

Think About It: *Some groups are not treated fairly. Then is anyone really free?*

[CHALLENGING STATES]

It was 2013. Some same-sex couples wanted to marry. But their states said no. Same-sex marriage was not legal. The couples sued. They were from four states. (*Obergefell v. Hodges*) Some couples had gotten married in other states. It was legal in some places. But they wanted their marriages to be legal at home.

At the center was the 14th Amendment. It is about equal protection. And due process. Other couples sued too. They did so under the civil rights act. Did the state laws violate their rights? Trial courts said yes. The appeals court said no. The Supreme Court said it would hear the case.

[A SPLIT COURT]

Lawyers stood before the justices. They were from both sides. Each presented their case. The justices sat. They listened. Should the states allow same-sex couples to marry? Yes. That's what one lawyer said. "Gay and lesbian people are equal. They deserve equal protection of the laws ..."

Are the states ignoring the rights of gays and lesbians? No. That's what another lawyer said. "The state doesn't have an interest in love and emotion at all."

The justices were split. Four agreed with the couples. Four did not. It was now up to Justice Kennedy. He would break the tie.

[5–4 RULING]

It was a hot June day. The court had made a decision. Same-sex marriage was legal in every state. The court voted 5–4. Justice Kennedy agreed. He spoke for the court. All people had the right to marry. The Constitution said so. It made them equal, he said.

Kennedy wrote a great opinion. The Constitution promises liberty. It makes this promise to all citizens. He said that marriage was a bond. And through marriage, couples find other freedoms.

The justice said laws have to change. Why? Because people change. This was one of those times. The due process clause is clear. No state should "deprive any person of life, liberty, or property, without due process of law." Kennedy said personal dignity was key to due process. And all people are allowed dignity.

[CHEERS AND BOOS]

It was a big decision. Historic. People ran into the streets. Some cheered. Others cried. Same-sex couples were the same as any husband and wife. They would have all the rights that go with marriage. They could share property. Health insurance. Bank accounts. Custody of children.

Some people were upset. They did not like the ruling. Justice Roberts wrote the **dissent**. The court was wrong, he said. He listed the reasons. Roberts said voters should change marriage laws. It was not up to the court.

FACES IN THE CROWD

John G. Roberts Jr.
Born: January 27, 1955

John Roberts is the chief justice. President George W. Bush gave him the job. It was in 2005. Congress okayed it. Roberts was the youngest chief justice in 100 years. In college he wanted to be a history teacher. But then he went to law school. Roberts loved the law. He became a lawyer. Roberts later became chief justice. He also oversees three circuit courts.

[GAME CHANGERS]

The justices' rulings have lasting value. They can change the U.S. forever. That's what happened with three justices. John Marshall's court was first. It ruled on *Marbury v. Madison*. Charles Evans Hughes stood up to President Franklin D. Roosevelt. Some programs under the New Deal were not legal. Earl Warren's court struck down Jim Crow laws. Joseph Story. William Brennan Jr. Oliver Wendell Holmes Jr. John Marshall Harlan. Hugo Black. Louis Brandeis. These men had ideas about the future. They thought beyond the limits of their own lifetime.

When we lose the right to be different, we lose the privilege to be free.

—Charles Evans Hughes

GLOSSARY

admonished: advised to do something

appealed: a request made to a higher court or authority to review the case

backlash: a strong reaction against something

boycott: to refuse to do something as a form of protest

civil rights: basic rights, such as voting or being treated fairly by the law

dissent: to disagree

inherently: built-in as a part of something

judicial review: the courts can say that a law is not legal; it is against the U.S. Constitution

justices: judges in a court of law

landmark: a very important event

majority opinion: the written court ruling issued by the greatest number of judges who voted one way or another

overrode: to disregard something; to make something no longer binding

overturned: to decide that something is wrong and make it different or invalid

precedents: court cases that can be used to justify a separate ruling

racism: a belief that one group of people is better than another because of their race

ruling: the decision of a judge

solicitor general: the person directly below the attorney general; responsible for representing the executive branch's interests in the Supreme Court

stare decisis: following the rules set down by the court's prior decisions when reviewing a new case

verdict: the decision of a jury

writ of certiorari: an order of a higher court to reexamine a lower court's ruling

PRIMARY SOURCES

[A LOOK AT THE PAST]

What is a primary source? It is a document. Or a piece of art. Or an artifact. It was created in the past. A primary source can answer questions. It can also lead to more questions. Three primary sources are included in this book. **The Preamble to the U.S. Constitution**. It explains why the framers chose to create a republic. **The Bill of Rights**. It guarantees certain freedoms. And the **Declaration of Independence**. It stresses natural rights. More can be found at the National Archives (online at *archives.gov.*) These sources were written for the people. (That means us.) The people broke free from the king's tyranny. The United States of America was born. Read the primary sources. Be an eyewitness to history.

We the people of the United States, in order to form a more perfect Union, establish justice, insure domestic Tranquility, provide for the common defense, promote the general welfare, and secure the blessings of liberty to ourselves and our posterity, do ordain and establish this Constitution for the United States of America.

[PREAMBLE]

THE U.S. BILL OF RIGHTS

THE PREAMBLE TO THE BILL OF RIGHTS

CONGRESS OF THE UNITED STATES begun and held at the City of New York, Wednesday, March 4, 1789.

THE Conventions of a number of the states, having at the time of their adopting the Constitution, expressed a desire, in order to prevent misconstruction or abuse of its powers, that further declaratory and restrictive clauses should be added: And as extending the ground of public confidence in the government, will best ensure the beneficent ends of its institution.

RESOLVED by the Senate and House of Representatives of the United States of America, in Congress assembled, two-thirds of both Houses concurring, that the following Articles be proposed to the legislatures of the several states, as amendments to the Constitution of the United States, all, or any of which articles, when ratified by three-fourths of the said legislatures, to be valid to all intents and purposes, as part of the said Constitution; viz.

ARTICLES in addition to, and amendment of the Constitution of the United States of America, proposed by Congress, and ratified by the legislatures of the several states, pursuant to the fifth article of the original Constitution.

AMENDMENT I

Congress shall make no law respecting an establishment of religion, or prohibiting the free exercise thereof; or abridging the freedom of speech, or of the press; or the right of the people peaceably to assemble, and to petition the government for a redress of grievances.

AMENDMENT II

A well regulated militia, being necessary to the security of a free state, the right of the people to keep and bear arms, shall not be infringed.

AMENDMENT III

No soldier shall, in time of peace be quartered in any house, without the consent of the owner, nor in time of war, but in a manner to be prescribed by law.

AMENDMENT IV

The right of the people to be secure in their persons, houses, papers, and effects, against unreasonable searches and seizures, shall not be violated, and no warrants shall issue, but upon probable cause, supported by oath or affirmation, and particularly describing the place to be searched, and the persons or things to be seized.

AMENDMENT V

No person shall be held to answer for a capital, or otherwise infamous crime, unless on a presentment or indictment of a grand jury, except in cases arising in the land or naval forces, or in the militia, when in actual service in time of war or public danger; nor shall any person be subject for the same offense to be twice put in jeopardy of life or limb; nor shall be compelled in any criminal case to be a witness against himself, nor be deprived of life, liberty, or property, without due process of law; nor shall private property be taken for public use, without just compensation.

AMENDMENT VI

In all criminal prosecutions, the accused shall enjoy the right to a speedy and public trial, by an impartial jury of the state and district wherein the crime shall have been committed, which district shall have been previously ascertained by law, and to be informed of the nature and cause of the accusation; to be confronted with the witnesses against him; to have compulsory process for obtaining witnesses in his favor, and to have the assistance of counsel for his defense.

AMENDMENT VII

In suits at common law, where the value in controversy shall exceed 20 dollars, the right of trial by jury shall be preserved, and no fact tried by a jury, shall be otherwise re-examined in any court of the United States, than according to the rules of the common law.

AMENDMENT VIII

Excessive bail shall not be required, nor excessive fines imposed, nor cruel and unusual punishments inflicted.

AMENDMENT IX

The enumeration in the Constitution, of certain rights, shall not be construed to deny or disparage others retained by the people.

AMENDMENT X

The powers not delegated to the United States by the Constitution, nor prohibited by it to the states, are reserved to the states respectively, or to the people.

IN CONGRESS, JULY 4, 1776.

The unanimous Declaration of the thirteen United States of America,

When in the course of human events, it becomes necessary for one people to dissolve the political bands which have connected them with another, and to assume among the powers of the earth, the separate and equal station to which the laws of nature and of nature's god entitle them, a decent respect to the opinions of mankind requires that they should declare the causes which impel them to the separation.

&◦◦&

We hold these truths to be self-evident, that all men are created equal, that they are endowed by their Creator with certain unalienable rights, that among these are life, liberty and the pursuit of happiness. That to secure these rights, governments are instituted among men, deriving their just powers from the consent of the governed. That whenever any form of government becomes destructive of these ends, it is the right of the people to alter or to abolish it, and to institute new government, laying its foundation on such principles and organizing its powers in such form, as to them shall seem most likely to effect their safety and happiness. Prudence, indeed, will dictate that governments long established should not be changed for light and transient causes; and accordingly all experience has shown, that mankind are more disposed to suffer, while evils are sufferable, than to right themselves by abolishing the forms to which they are accustomed. But when a long train of abuses and usurpations, pursuing invariably the same object evinces a design to reduce them under absolute despotism, it is their right, it is their duty, to throw off such government, and to provide new guards for their future security. Such has been the patient sufferance of these colonies; and such is now the necessity which constrains them to alter their former systems of government. The history of the present king of Great Britain is a history of repeated injuries and usurpations, all having in direct object the establishment of an absolute tyranny over these states. To prove this, let facts be submitted to a candid world.

He has refused his assent to laws, the most wholesome and necessary for the public good.

He has forbidden his governors to pass laws of immediate and pressing importance, unless suspended in their operation till his assent should be obtained; and when so suspended, he has utterly neglected to attend to them.

He has refused to pass other laws for the accommodation of large districts of people, unless those people would relinquish the right of representation in the legislature, a right inestimable to them and formidable to tyrants only.

He has called together legislative bodies at places unusual, uncomfortable, and distant from the depository of their public records, for the sole purpose of fatiguing them into compliance with his measures.

He has dissolved representative houses repeatedly, for opposing with manly firmness his invasions on the rights of the people.

He has refused for a long time, after such dissolutions, to cause others to be elected; whereby the legislative powers, incapable of annihilation, have returned to the people at large for their exercise; the state remaining in the mean time exposed to all the dangers of invasion from without, and convulsions within.

He has endeavored to prevent the population of these states; for that purpose obstructing the laws for naturalization of foreigners; refusing to pass others to encourage their migrations hither, and raising the conditions of new appropriations of lands.

He has obstructed the administration of justice, by refusing his assent to laws for establishing judiciary powers.

He has made judges dependent on his will alone, for the tenure of their offices, and the amount and payment of their salaries.

He has erected a multitude of new offices, and sent hither swarms of officers to harrass our people, and eat out their substance.

He has kept among us, in times of peace, standing armies without the consent of our legislatures.

He has affected to render the military independent of and superior to the civil power.

He has combined with others to subject us to a jurisdiction foreign to our constitution, and unacknowledged by our laws; giving his assent to their acts of pretended legislation:

For quartering large bodies of armed troops among us;

For protecting them, by a mock trial, from punishment for any murders which they should commit on the inhabitants of these states;

For cutting off our trade with all parts of the world;

For imposing taxes on us without our consent;

For depriving us in many cases, of the benefits of trial by jury;

For transporting us beyond seas to be tried for pretended offenses;

For abolishing the free system of English laws in a neighboring province, establishing therein an arbitrary government, and enlarging its boundaries so as to render it at once an example and fit instrument for introducing the same absolute rule into these colonies;

For taking away our charters, abolishing our most valuable laws, and altering fundamentally the forms of our governments;

For suspending our own legislatures, and declaring themselves invested with power to legislate for us in all cases whatsoever.

He has abdicated government here, by declaring us out of his protection and waging war against us.

He has plundered our seas, ravaged our coasts, burnt our towns, and destroyed the lives of our people.

He is at this time transporting large armies of foreign mercenaries to complete the works of death, desolation and tyranny, already begun with circumstances of cruelty and perfidy scarcely paralleled in the most barbarous ages, and totally unworthy the head of a civilized nation.

He has constrained our fellow citizens taken captive on the high seas to bear arms against their country, to become the executioners of their friends and brethren, or to fall themselves by their hands.

He has excited domestic insurrections amongst us, and has endeavored to bring on the inhabitants of our frontiers, the merciless Indian savages, whose known rule of warfare, is an undistinguished destruction of all ages, sexes and conditions.

In every stage of these oppressions we have petitioned for redress in the most humble terms: our repeated petitions have been answered only by repeated injury. A prince whose character is thus marked by every act which may define a tyrant, is unfit to be the ruler of a free people.

Nor have we been wanting in attentions to our Brittish brethren. We have warned them from time to time of attempts by their legislature to extend an unwarrantable jurisdiction over us. We have reminded them of the circumstances of our emigration and settlement here. We have appealed to their native justice and magnanimity, and we have conjured them by the ties of our common kindred to disavow these usurpations, which, would inevitably interrupt our connections and correspondence. They too have been deaf to the voice of justice and of consanguinity. We must, therefore, acquiesce in the necessity, which denounces our separation, and hold them, as we hold the rest of mankind, enemies in war, in peace friends.

We, therefore, the representatives of the United States of America, in General Congress, assembled, appealing to the Supreme Judge of the world for the rectitude of our intentions, do, in the name, and by authority of the good people of these colonies, solemnly publish and declare, that these united colonies are, and of right ought to be free and independent states; that they are absolved from all allegiance to the British Crown, and that all political connection between them and the state of Great Britain, is and ought to be totally dissolved; and that as free and independent states, they have full power to levy war, conclude peace, contract alliances, establish commerce, and to do all other acts and things which independent states may of right do. And for the support of this declaration, with a firm reliance on the protection of divine providence, we mutually pledge to each other our lives, our fortunes and our sacred honor.

There are 56 signatures on the Declaration. They appear in six columns.

COLUMN 1

GEORGIA

Button Gwinnett

Lyman Hall

George Walton

COLUMN 2

NORTH CAROLINA

William Hooper

Joseph Hewes

John Penn

SOUTH CAROLINA

Edward Rutledge

Thomas Heyward, Jr.

Thomas Lynch, Jr.

Arthur Middleton

COLUMN 3

MASSACHUSETTS

John Hancock

MARYLAND

Samuel Chase

William Paca

Thomas Stone

Charles Carroll of Carrollton

VIRGINIA

George Wythe

Richard Henry Lee

Thomas Jefferson

Benjamin Harrison

Thomas Nelson, Jr.

Francis Lightfoot Lee

Carter Braxton

COLUMN 4

PENNSYLVANIA

Robert Morris

Benjamin Rush

Benjamin Franklin

John Morton

George Clymer

James Smith

George Taylor

James Wilson

George Ross

DELAWARE

Caesar Rodney

George Read

Thomas McKean

COLUMN 5

NEW YORK

William Floyd

Philip Livingston

Francis Lewis

Lewis Morris

NEW JERSEY

Richard Stockton

John Witherspoon

Francis Hopkinson

John Hart

Abraham Clark

COLUMN 6

NEW HAMPSHIRE

Josiah Bartlett

William Whipple

MASSACHUSETTS

Samuel Adams

John Adams

Robert Treat Paine

Elbridge Gerry

RHODE ISLAND

Stephen Hopkins

William Ellery

CONNECTICUT

Roger Sherman

Samuel Huntington

William Williams

Oliver Wolcott

NEW HAMPSHIRE

Matthew Thornton

[DECLARATION OF INDEPENDENCE]

Be an engaged citizen in today's world.
Meet life's challenges after high school. Are
you fully prepared for democratic decision
making? Do you know how to address
and approach issues in a democratic
and responsible way? These five unique
handbooks will show you how.

AMERICAN GOVERNMENT

American Government
FOUNDATIONS
John Perritano

9781680211184

American Government
OFFICE OF THE PRESIDENT
John Perritano

9781680211214

American Government
CONGRESS
John Perritano

9781680211207

American Government
SUPREME COURT
John Perritano

9781680211191

American Government
POLITICAL PARTIES
John Perritano

9781680211221